Tropical Cocktails

AND MIXED DRINKS

Tropical Cocktails
AND MIXED DRINKS

Created and Selected by MIKE HENRY

Ward Lock Limited · London

ACKNOWLEDGEMENTS

I would like to pay special thanks to my friend Gregg Lee whose idea for a Caribbean drinks book it was; to the numerous bartenders throughout the Caribbean who generously contributed their recipes; and to Ray Chen whose superb photography enlivens and enhances the drinks; to Mr. Claude Fortier, Master-Bar-Tender, who interpreted some of my drinks for Ray Chen and added some of his own devising; and to my editor Liz Hearne whose assistance was more than invaluable.

M.H.

This edition first published in Great Britain in 1987
by Ward Lock Limited, 8 Clifford Street
London W1X 1RB, an Egmont Company

Designed by Wayne Chen
Photography by Ray Chen
Text set in Futura book

Printed and bound in Spain by Graficas Reunidas, S.A.

ISBN 07063 6498 8

CONTENTS

INTRODUCTION

The Caribbean has always conjured up for the northerners the image of relaxed, warm and exciting living – islands of swaying coconut trees, caressed by a tropical breeze, framed in a background of azure sea. Blue-green bedecked mountains are intermittently bathed by refreshing rains and washed by clean, clear streams. Here the fingers of nature work to produce rich crops of sugar-cane, bananas, coconuts, ginger, coffee, cinnamon, pimento and cloves. Here too are the exotic fruits of pineapple, mango, passion fruit, papaya and the more familiar orange and grapefruit. Each of these when processed or blended has, over the years, provided the imbibers of the world with some of the most widely used and enjoyed drinks and cocktails – yet all unacknowledged.

To compensate for this neglect, I have presented in these pages a combination of Caribbean and international cocktails which tantalizingly capture the warmth and flavour of the Islands, reflecting the creativity of the bartenders and alcohol producers of the region.

All that's left, then, to complement this creativity is for you to buy the book, pick up the ingredients at your friendly liquor store and head home. Switch on the stereo and caress the mind with your favourite music (Caribbean, preferably reggae or calypso). Invite that special friend – or friends – over, mix, stir, blend and shake the captivating flavours and let the natural charm of the Caribbean take over…

Simply put, that's what dreams are made from. I can attest to that for that's how this book came about.

STOCK AND SUPPLIES FOR A BASIC BAR

The basic Caribbean bar should include white, light and dark rums, rum punch, 151° rum and aged rums. Also essential are rum based liqueurs, coffee liqueurs, pimento liqueurs and other regional specialties. Curaçao, or Triple Sec, Campari and Angostura bitters must be included.

To complete the bar, one must stock Scotch, rye and bourbon whiskies, brandy, gin, vodka, vermouth (both sweet and dry), plus other basic liqueurs such as Avocaat, cherry brandy, crème de cacao, crème de menthe, both green and white, Cointreau and Drambuie.

For soft drinks, there should be cola, Jamaican dry ginger ale, soda water and tonic water. Simple syrup can easily be made by boiling two parts of sugar with one part of water for five minutes. Allow this to cool and keep bottled in the refrigerator for use as needed. A range of juices is necessary, from papaya, mango and pineapple to orange, grapefruit, lemon, lime and tomato.

Listed below are perishable and other items to be kept on hand for the well-supplied bar.

Lemons	Consommé	Nutmeg
Limes	Black Pepper	Cinnamon
Oranges	Cayenne	Mint
Maraschino cherries	Salt	Cucumber
Olives	Sugar	Eggs
Cocktail onions	Cloves	Cream

BASIC BAR EQUIPMENT

Cocktail shaker
Mixing glass
Electric blender
Ice bucket and tongs
Ice pick
Bar spoon
Openers (bottle and
    can)

Corkscrew
Sharp knife
Chopping board
Lime squeezer
Strainer
Lemon peeler
Nutmeg grater

Straws
Toothpicks
Swizzle sticks
Coasters
Napkins
Cloth for glasses

TIPS FOR MAKING GOOD DRINKS

- Always measure your ingredients. Don't guess.

- Always try to present a cocktail as attractively as possible.

- Use clean, unchipped glasses.

- If possible, serve all drinks in chilled glasses. Place glasses in the freezing compartment of the refrigerator for a few minutes or place a few cubes of ice in them prior to mixing the drink. Discard this ice before serving.

- To frost glasses, put them into the freezer while wet.

- Serve drinks ice cold. Have plenty of fresh ice on hand.

- Always use freshly made ice for each round of drinks.

- Put ice into glass, shaker or mixer first to chill ingredients quickly except for recipes using sugar, which then comes first.

- In simple drinks, ice comes first, then liquor, then mix.

- Stir all clear drinks, e.g. Martinis, with ice before straining into glass.

- Drinks containing ingredients such as fruit juices or cream, e.g. Whisky Sour or Brandy Alexander, should be shaken hard to achieve a perfect blend. They can also be whirled in an electric blender.

- Use fresh juices whenever possible.

- For a 'frothy collar' on drinks, add a tablespoon of egg white before shaking.

- Soda water and all carbonated beverages should be chilled and added last.

- Use only the 'zest', the green or yellow part of the lemon/lime/orange, whenever peel is required. Do not include the pith, the white bitter membrane of the rind.

- Add peel, cherry or other fruit after the drink has been shaken or mixed.

- Do not overload drinks with garnishing.

- Serve the cocktail as soon as possible after mixing.

MEASUREMENTS

In the USA, the smallest practical unit of liquid capacity is the liquid ounce. In the UK, it is the slightly larger fluid ounce (fl oz) although, thanks to the EEC, this is now giving way to the centilitre (cl) of Western Europe.

Cocktail glasses vary in capacity from 2 to 3½ ounces. The average UK size is 2½ ounces.

The 4 ounce wine glass (USA) is a good size for sours such as vodka and tomato juice.

The 5 ounce wine glass is one of the UK sizes.

SOME METRIC EQUIVALENTS

14 cl	= 5 fluid ounces	= 1 noggin
23 cl	= 8 ounce wine glass (UK)	
28.4 cl	= 10 fluid ounces	= 1 half-pint (UK)
33 cl	= 12 ounce wine glass	
55 cl	= 20 fluid ounces	= 1 pint (UK)
75 cl	= 1 reputed quart	= usual wine bottle size
100 cl	= 1 litre	
1.14 l	= 40 fluid ounces	= 20 gills (UK)
	= 1 Imperial quart	= ¼ Imperial gallon

SOME STANDARD UK BAR MEASURES

1 dessert spoon = ½ fluid ounce
6 out measure = ⅚ fluid ounce
5 out measure = 1 fluid ounce
4 out measure = 1¾ fluid ounces
1 gill   = 2 fluid ounces

SOME STANDARD USA BAR MEASURES

1 dash   = 6 drops
1 teaspoon = ⅙ ounce
1 tablespoon = ½ ounce
1 pony   = 1 ounce
1 jigger   = 1½ ounces
1 large jigger = 2 ounces
1 wine glass = 4 ounces   = 1 gill
1 split   = 6 ounces
1 cup   = 8 ounces
1 pint   = 16 ounces
1 fifth   = 25.6 ounces
1 quart   = 32 ounces

CONVERSION TABLE

To change from	To	Multiply by
grams	ounces	0.035
ounces	grams	28.35
kilograms	pounds	2.205
pounds	kilograms	0.454
centilitres	fluid ounces (UK)	0.352
	liquid ounces (USA)	0.338
gallons (UK)	litres	4.50
gallons (USA)	litres	3.80
litres	decilitres	10.00

Temperature:

°F to °C deduct 31 and multiply by $\frac{5}{9}$.
°C to °F multiply by $\frac{9}{5}$ and add 32.

OUR CARIBBEAN PRODUCTS

Rum and the Caribbean have long had an inseparable association. Although rum has a history going back to Roman times and although it has been produced from China to Italy, only in the West Indies has the perfect combination of sugar-cane, climate and skill brought rum production to its peak.

The sugar-cane from which rum is made was brought from the Canaries to Jamaica by Christopher Columbus himself in 1494. Rum was to become the drink of the slaves on the plantations of the Caribbean and of the seamen of the British Royal Navy. After Admirals Penn and Venables had captured Jamaica in 1655, they took its heavy, dark rum back to Britain where it became so popular that it was ultimately established as the Navy's official drink, every hand being issued his daily tot for well over two hundred years.

The making of rum and sugar starts from the same point. Freshly cut sugar-cane is crushed between huge rollers and the juice which is extracted is clarified in large vats. The sugar is taken off by further processing, leaving behind the molasses which is the base for almost all Caribbean rums. Yeast and water are added to the molasses to bring about fermentation which is followed by distillation, aging and blending, the final stage of preparation.

Rum is considered to be superior to vodka, whisky or gin because sugar is already present in the cane, eliminating the need for a preliminary malting process necessary to convert starch to sugar. Rum retains its rich, natural flavour, unless further processing lightens it.

Of all the spirits, rum is perhaps one of the 'hottest'. The traditional dark, pungent, heavy-bodied rums of Jamaica fall definitely into this hot category while the odourless and almost colourless ones, mostly from Cuba and Puerto Rico, form a light, cool contrast. However, a wide variety of rums spans these two extremes, modified by production methods and blending. The lighter, middle-range rums are dry and very versatile.

For cocktails, a light-bodied or white rum is often best. Hot drinks are ideal with a heavier Jamaican or Demerara rum. And rum of any kind blends well with fruit juices and most liqueurs.

In recent years, the liqueurs of the Caribbean have been increasing in number and becoming more widely appreciated. Delicately flavoured Curaçao from the island of the same name has long been a favourite, whether white or blue, and coffee liqueurs, not only Tia Maria, are standard in any bar. Tropical flavours, banana, coconut and pineapple, are used in the long-established Barbancourt liqueurs from Haiti, and Ole Nassau liqueurs produced in the Bahamas. These are rum based as are most Caribbean liqueurs. Jamaica produces a unique rum liqueur, Rumona, the only one in the world. Also from Jamaica come Sangster's Old Jamaica Liqueurs. Produced high in the Blue Mountains, these international prize winners include such unusual flavours as ortanique, coffee-orange and pimento. Barbados has the delicate Falernum. Almost every larger island has a liqueur it calls its own.

Trinidad is the present-day home of Angostura bitters, indisputably world famous. Originally compounded in about 1825 by the French Dr Siegert to combat disease among Bolivar's troops in Venezuela, its formula has remained unchanged ever since, although its main function now is as an indispensable ingredient in many cocktails and mixed drinks.

Finally, and perhaps surprisingly, Campari is closely linked with the West Indies. An essential ingredient of this bitter-sweet Italian aperitif is a nut supposedly found only in the Bahamas. What a contribution the Caribbean has made to the bars of the world.

THE MAKING OF RUM

In the Caribbean, rum is usually made from molasses, a by-product of sugar manufacture, although it can be made from sugar-cane juice or a combination of the two. All three bases have the advantage of containing their own, natural sugar so that the essential process of fermentation can take place without the addition of any other form of starch for the yeast to work upon.

As with any liquor, rum is the final result of a series of complex processes, in this case, fermentation, distillation, aging and blending.

During fermentation, yeast converts sugar into alcohol and carbon dioxide. Before this process begins, however, the molasses is diluted with water to bring the sugar content down to 15%, pasteurized and pumped into fermenting tanks of up to 24,000 gallons capacity. Meanwhile, a yeast culture is prepared, reaching 2,000 gallons, which is enough to tackle the 26,000 lbs of dissolved sugar in the fermenter. The yeast, molasses and water mixture is called the 'live wash', a name justified by the bubbles and motion appearing on the surface of the liquid while the yeast converts the sugar into 3,000 gallons of alcohol and 13,000 lbs of carbon dioxide. It can take as little as thirty hours for all the sugar to be converted, at which point the yeast will die from lack of nutrient. The 'dead wash' is then ready for distillation.

There are two distinct methods of distillation, but the purpose of each is the same: to separate the alcohol from the rest of the liquid in the dead wash. The two methods are the Pot Still and the Continuous or Column Still.

The pot still is the traditional, time-honoured method of distilling. It uses what is basically a steam heated kettle on a huge scale to distil by means of evaporation and condensation. Three condensates are recovered; rum, with an 85% alcohol content, high wine and low wine. The rum is put into storage tanks and the wines, which have lower concentrations of alcohol, are redistilled in the next cycle of the pot still.

The column or continuous still consists of three gigantic columns heated at the base by steam. The columns contain perforated trays through which steam can rise and downpipes to carry off the condensates. The first column strips the weak solution of alcohol from the wash, and the other two purify and concentrate the alcoholic vapours. These vapours condense on the top trays, the higher the purer, so that the condensate from the highest trays is pure alcohol which can be used in the manufacture of gin, vodka and liqueurs. Lower down the columns, a mild rum is formed.

With the refinement of the column still in recent years, the trend has been for rum distillers to replace their pot stills with column stills, so that now only a small percentage of the world's rum is produced in pot stills. This makes good economic sense since the pot still, essentially a small batch method, is slow and needs the art of a master distiller. The full body and subtle characteristics of the pot still rum develop only after long aging. The column still, by contrast, is a continuous process of distillation which can be run nonstop for months on end. The process is scientifically controlled and extremely efficient, giving a high yield of light-bodied rum which requires much less aging and so is much less costly. In the Caribbean, however, a significant number of rum producers use both pot and column stills, for while a column still can produce large quantities of excellent blending rum, there is no substitute for the taste and aroma that a well-aged pot still rum can give to a blend.

New rum is harsh to the taste. It needs to be aged for years before it is at its peak. Over the centuries, it has been discovered that rum ages best in 40 gallon oak casks which have been charred inside. The charred wood mellows the rum which is also able to 'breathe' because of the permeable nature of the oak. Breathing is important. It results in such complex chemical changes that by the time the rum leaves the barrel, it has developed a new taste and aroma. Anyone going through a rum warehouse will notice the pleasant smell and temperature caused by the evaporation of the rum. Aging is an expensive process because of the large quantities of stock held at that stage and the extensive warehousing needed. A pot still rum can take from five to twelve years to reach maturity. Column still rums rarely need more than three. In addition, evaporation causes the loss of some 6% of the contents of each barrel, sometimes known as 'the angels' share'. Loss of this kind is inevitable anywhere, but in a temperate climate it would be only 2%. Still, the price is worth paying since, after repeated experimentation, it has been found that only tropical aging can produce a mellow, smooth rum.

Finally, the blending stage is reached, a stage entirely dependent on the skill and experience of the blender. The contents of each barrel are tested and the chief blender decides on the proportions needed of the lighter column still rums and the richer pot still products. Each final formula is a closely guarded secret. When the rums have been combined, distilled water is used to dilute them to bottling strength. Caramel may be added to darken the colour, then the mixture rests for days in huge vats, a period known as the 'marrying of the blends'. At last, with the harmony of the blend guaranteed, the rum is ready for bottling.

Today, the most modern technology is used in the making of rum, from fermentation to bottling. Much of the process has been automated. But the human factor is irreplaceable, from the expert who selects a particular strain of yeast for fermentation to the master distiller and the blender whose 'nose' is the final arbiter. Without the presence of such skills and experience, the fine rums of the Caribbean could not have achieved the quality and consistency for which they are renowned.

RUMS OF THE ISLANDS

The Bahamas
For many years, the only rum products from these 700 scattered islands were the outstanding Ole Nassau Liqueurs, blended from imported rums and the finest tropical flavourings. Since the early sixties, however, the famous House of Bacardi has produced its characteristic light rum here as well as in Puerto Rico.

Barbados
This very British Caribbean island produces a lighter bodied rum, tending to medium. Many of the fine aged rums of Barbados can be drunk almost as liqueurs. The best known Barbados rum is Mount Gay.

Cuba
The largest of the Caribbean islands, Cuba was once the major supplier of light rums, including the renowned Bacardi. However, under the Castro government, exports ended and most of the major distillers moved to other parts of the Caribbean. Distillation in continuous stills from a molasses base produces a very light rum with a fragrant, refreshing taste. The two main rums are Carta Blanca and Carta Oro, a golden rum coloured with caramel.

French Guyana
Two types of white rum are produced at two distilleries, Mirande and Prevot, but these are almost totally for local consumption.

Guadeloupe
This island is one of the two major suppliers of French rums of the full-bodied, pot still type. Most of its production is shipped in bulk to France for further maturation and bottling. Some of the local distilleries producing rum are Tabanon, Longueteau, Routa, Bourdon, Bologne Lassere, Neron and Pères Blancs.

Guyana

Although Guyana is part of the Latin American mainland, its rums are classified as Caribbean. The most famous is Demerara, named after the river which irrigates most of the sugar-cane fields. Like the sugar which bears the same name, Demerara rum is dark and rich. Fermentation is rapid (48 hours the maximum), giving a lightness to the spirit. Close to Georgetown are distillers such as Enmore, Diamond, Versailles and Uitvlugt.

Haiti

The first independent negro nation, Haiti produces most of its cane in the shelter of high mountains on the northern hook of the island. The cane juice is distilled without being allowed to ferment. The double pot still method (the cognac method) gives the medium to full-bodied rums a considerable fragrance and moderate alcoholic strength.

Primary distillation gives a clear rum known locally as Clairin. It is used as a cheap drink and has an important part in voodoo rites as the libation offered to the spirit gods. The second distillation gives the true, full-flavoured, aromatic Haitian rum. Some of the main distilleries are Damien or Rhum Barbancourt (considered to be one of the finest Caribbean rums), Rhum Nazon, Rhum Tesserot and Rhum Champion.

Jamaica

Traditional Jamaican rums are full-flavoured, dark with a rich aroma. These rums, once commonly called Wedderburn and Plummer, were the rums supplied to the British Navy for over 200 years. Today, Jamaica produces a full range of rums from molasses. Light-flavoured rums are produced in column stills after a short fermentation. Medium-bodied pot still rums have cane juice mixed with the molasses to give a fine aroma. Heavy, slowly fermented pot still rums of the Wedderburn and Plummer types have a dark, rich fragrance.

The local rum drink is Whites – a strong, clean white rum consumed either straight or with any chaser from water through milk to Coke. In its first distillation, it is known as 'culu culu' and is often used locally to make rum punch of the strongest type. Among the best known brands are Myers, Charley's and Appleton which has been produced on the firm's own sugar estates since 1825.

Martinique
Home of the major French-based rums. Most of these are made from cane juice and are sold either without casking as Grappe Blanc or are matured to take on the colour of the wooden casks. Grappe Blanc is the main ingredient of Martinique's rum punch, a popular island drink. Major distilleries are Duquesne and Clement. The Martinique-type brands are Genippa, Grand Case, Val d'Or, (a ten-year old rum), Rhum Clement and Rhum St James. Others such as Vive, which is made from molasses only, are similar to the heavy Jamaican rums in flavour and aroma.

Puerto Rico
This island has replaced Cuba as the leading producer of white rums. Puerto Rican rums are traditionally distilled from molasses in a continuous still to a high strength while retaining lightness and a good aroma. In order to ensure their pale colour, Puerto Rican rums are very seldom stored in barrels. In addtion, to Bacardi, well-known rums are Ron Rico, Ron Viejo, Maraca, Vanioca and Don Q.

Trinidad
An oil producing, carnival country which makes good quality, medium-bodied rums from quick fermented molasses distilled in continuous stills. The alcoholic content is high. The most widely known brand is Old Oak.

Virgin Islands
The three islands, St Thomas, St John's and St Croix, make rums which are similar to the Trinidadian. They are sold under the brand name Cruzan.

RUM BASED DRINKS

BAHAMA MAMA

1¼ oz dark rum
3 oz pineapple juice
¼ oz lemon juice
¼ oz Angostura bitters
1 oz crème de cassis
3 oz orange juice
Dash of Grenadine
Dash of nutmeg

Shake well and serve in a tall glass with ice.

BANANA DAIQUIRI

1½ oz dark rum
1 tablespoon Curaçao
1½ oz lime juice
1 teaspoon sugar
1 medium sized banana, sliced
1 cup crushed ice

Combine all ingredients in a blender. Blend at low speed for five seconds then at high speed until mixture thickens. Pour into a champagne glass. Top with a cherry.

BIG BAMBOO

2 oz dark rum
¼ oz lime juice
¼ oz Grenadine
¼ oz Triple Sec
1 oz orange juice

Shake well with ice. Strain into a large mug or tall glass packed with powdered ice. Garnish with pineapple, a sprig of mint and serve with a straw.

BLACK ROSE

1½ oz dark rum
1 teaspoon sugar
Cold black coffee

Place the sugar in a tall glass and stir in the rum. Add ice and fill up with coffee.

BUCCANEER MARY

2 oz white rum
4¼ oz tomato juice
¾ oz lime juice
3 or 4 dashes Worcestershire sauce
3 or 4 drops Tabasco sauce
Salt

Stir with cracked ice. Strain into 2 cocktail glasses. Serve with a sprinkle of black pepper.

BUCCANEER PUNCH

3 oz dark rum
1 oz lime juice
3 teaspoons sugar
Dash of Angostura bitters
1 cup cracked ice

Shake well and pour unstrained into glass. Add a slice of lime and a little nutmeg. Serve with a straw. For tall drinks, top up with soda water.

CARNIVAL JUMP-UP

2 oz dark rum
½ oz Grenadine
½ oz fresh lime juice
1 oz fresh coconut cream
Slice of pineapple
Slice of lime

Shake all liquids with ice and pour into a small Bengali glass. Garnish with pineapple and lime. Serves 2.

CHINESE COCKTAIL

1½ oz dark rum
1 tablespoon Grenadine
1 dash bitters
1 teaspoon Maraschino
1 teaspoon Triple Sec

Shake with ice and strain into a cocktail glass.

CLARENDON COCKTAIL

1½ oz dark rum
Juice of 1 lime
3 teaspoons powdered sugar
1 oz grapefruit juice
1 dash bitters

Shake with ice and strain into a cocktail glass.

COCONUT OAK

1¼ oz dark rum
½ oz gin
½ oz Carypton
½ oz fresh lime juice
2 oz coconut water/milk
½ oz simple syrup
2 dashes Angostura bitters
½ coconut shell

Shake all ingredients with crushed ice. Serve in a coconut shell with straws and a hibiscus blossom. Serves 6.

CREOLE AMBER

1 oz amber rum
1 oz dark rum
½ oz orange juice
½ oz simple syrup
1 cherry
Slice of lime
½ oz Carypton
2 dashes Grenadine syrup
1 dash fresh coconut cream
Sprig of mint

Shake all liquids with crushed ice, then strain into a tall glass. Garnish with mint, the slice of lime and cherry.

CUBAN COCKTAIL

2 oz dark rum
1½ oz powdered sugar
Juice of ½ lime

Shake with ice and strain into a cocktail glass.

DAIQUIRI BERMUDA

1½ oz white rum
½ oz lemon or lime juice
1 teaspoon simple syrup

Shake well with ice. Strain into a chilled glass and serve with a short straw.

DIP-AN'-FALL-BACK

2 oz dark rum
½ teaspoon Curaçao
1 teaspoon orange juice
1 teaspoon lemon juice
1 teaspoon raspberry juice

Shake with ice and strain into a cocktail glass. Decorate with small slice of pineapple.

DOCTOR FUNK

½ oz dark rum
1 teaspoon Pernod
½ oz lemon juice
1 teaspoon Grenadine
¼ teaspoon sugar
1 lime

Cut lime in half and squeeze into shaker, dropping in the rinds also. Add all other ingredients and shake with crushed ice. Strain into a 12 ounce glass. If necessary, fill with soda water. Decorate with fruit, if desired.

EL PRESIDENTE

1½ oz light rum
½ oz Curaçao
½ oz dry vermouth
1 dash Grenadine

Shake well with ice and strain into a cocktail glass.

FISH HOUSE PUNCH

A celebrated Philadelphia Club recipe of 1732.

12 oz sugar
3 pints water
1½ pints lemon juice
1 bottle light rum
1 bottle dark rum
4½ oz peach brandy
1 bottle brandy

Dissolve the sugar in a little water in the punch bowl. Add the lemon and the rest of the water, stirring well. Add the rum, brandy and peach brandy. Stir and allow to stand for several hours. Before serving, put a big block of ice in the bowl. Serve when cold. Serves 25 to 30.

FROZEN DAIQUIRI (Stella's Joy)

6 oz light rum
1 tablespoon fresh lime juice
2 tablespoons powdered
  sugar
1/3 cup mango slices
  or
1/3 cup pineapple slices
2 cups crushed ice

Place crushed ice in blender. Add ingredients, starting with the rum. Blend on high until the consistency is like snow. Serve in 4 oz wine glasses with a straw. Top with a cherry.

GOOMBAY NIGHT

1¼ oz dark rum
¾ oz coconut rum
3 oz pineapple juice
¼ oz lemon juice
¼ oz Triple Sec
Dash of simple syrup

Shake well and serve over cracked ice in a tall glass. Garnish with a cherry and a slice of lemon.

GUADELOUPE

¾ oz dark rum
1½ oz pineapple juice
½ teaspoon lemon juice

Shake with ice and strain into a cocktail glass.

HIGH WIND

2 oz amber rum
1 oz pineapple juice
½ oz lime juice
1 oz Grenadine
½ oz orange juice

Shake well with ice and strain into a cocktail glass. Serve with a slice of orange.

HURRICANE

1 oz dark rum
1 oz light rum
1 tablespoon passion fruit
  syrup
2 teaspoons lime juice

Shake with ice and strain into a cocktail glass.

KINGSTON No. 1

1½ oz dark rum
½ oz Kummel
1½ oz orange juice
1 dash pimento dram

Shake with ice and strain into a cocktail glass.

KIN-PUPPA-LICK

1½ oz rum
1½ oz crème de menthe
  (white)
1 dash lemon juice

Shake with ice and strain into a cocktail glass.

LIMBO

1½ oz dark rum
½ teaspoon crème de menthe
½ teaspoon Curaçao
1 tablespoon lime juice
1 teaspoon powdered sugar

Shake with ice and strain into a cocktail glass. Add a slice of lime.

LIMEY

1 oz amber rum
1 oz lime liqueur
½ oz Curaçao
2 teaspoons lime juice

Combine ingredients with half a cup of crushed ice in blender. Blend at low speed and pour into a champagne glass. Add a twist of lime peel.

MAI-TAI

2 oz dark rum
1 oz Curaçao
1 tablespoon lime juice
½ teaspoon powdered sugar
1 tablespoon Orgeat or
   almond-flavoured syrup
1 tablespoon Grenadine

Shake with ice and strain into
a large old-fashioned glass
about ⅓ full of crushed ice.
Decorate with a maraschino
cherry speared to a wedge of
fruit, preferably fresh
pineapple. For a 'hair raiser',
top with a dash of 100°
proof rum, and for a real
Caribbean/Hawaiian effect,
float an orchid on each drink.
Serve with straws.

MORNING ROSE

¾ oz light rum
¾ oz Curaçao
½ oz Grenadine
½ oz lemon juice

Shake well and pour into a
cocktail glass.

MYRTLE BANK PUNCH

1½ oz Demerara rum, 151°
   proof
Juice of ½ lime
1 teaspoon sugar
6 dashes Grenadine
Maraschino

Combine in shaker with large
piece of ice. Shake and pour

over cracked ice in a
10-ounce glass. Float
Maraschino liqueur on top.

NAKED LADY

1½ oz light rum
1½ oz sweet vermouth
4 dashes apricot brandy
2 dashes Grenadine
4 dashes lemon juice

Shake well with ice and strain
into a cocktail glass.

NATIONAL

2 oz light rum
½ oz pineapple juice
½ oz apricot brandy
1 cherry

Shake well with shaved ice
and strain into a cocktail
glass. Serve with pineapple
stick or wedge and cherry.

OLYMPIA

1½ oz dark rum
1 oz cherry brandy
Juice of ½ lime

Shake well with ice and strain
into a cocktail glass.

PASSION DAIQUIRI

1½ oz dark rum
1 tablespoon passion fruit juice
1 teaspoon powdered sugar
Juice of 1 lime

Shake with ice and strain into
a cocktail glass.

PILOT HOUSE HOTEL PLANTER'S PUNCH

1¼ oz dark rum
3 oz pineapple juice
3 oz orange juice
¼ oz lemon juice
¼ oz Grenadine
¼ oz Angostura bitters
Dash of nutmeg

Shake well and serve in a tall
glass over ice.

PIÑA COLADA

3 oz amber rum
3 tablespoons coconut
   water/milk
3 tablespoons crushed
   pineapple

Place in blender with two
cups of crushed ice and
blend at high speed for a
short time. Strain into a
Tropical glass. Garnish with
fruits and serve with a straw.

PINEAPPLE FLING

1 oz amber rum
1 tablespoon lime juice
1 teaspoon Grenadine
1 teaspoon fresh cream

Shake with ice and strain into
a cocktail glass. Add a black
cherry soaked in rum.

33

PINEAPPLE RUM COCKTAIL

1½ oz amber rum
¾ oz pineapple juice
½ teaspoon lemon juice

Shake with ice and strain into a cocktail glass.

PIRATE'S PUNCH

2 oz dark rum
1 oz sweet vermouth
1 dash Angostura bitters

Stir well with ice and strain into a cocktail glass. Add a twist of lemon and serve.

PLANTER'S COCKTAIL

1½ oz dark rum
½ teaspoon powdered sugar
Juice of 1 lemon

Shake with ice and strain into a cocktail glass.

PLANTER'S PUNCH

3 parts dark rum
1 part lime juice
2 parts simple syrup
3 parts water, including ice or
   soda
1 dash of Curaçao or
   Angostura bitters (optional)

Starting with the syrup and lime juice, stir ingredients together well. Serve in a tall glass with cherries and orange slices. Each Caribbean island makes this drink with its own native rum.

POLICEMAN'S GLOW

4½ oz amber rum
1 pint Red Stripe beer (lager)
1 tin pineapple juice
Pinch of nutmeg or cinnamon

Mix all ingredients together and shake well. Pour over crushed ice in old-fashioned glasses. Garnish with orange or pineapple slice. Serves six.

PORT ROYAL

1 oz amber rum
1 oz Jamaican coffee liqueur
1 teaspoon lime juice

Serve over ice. Sip and listen for the sunken Port Royal church bells to ring.

PUERTO RICO MIX

1½ oz light rum
1 oz dark rum
1 teaspoon Absinthe substitute
¼ teaspoon Grenadine
1 tablespoon lemon juice
1 tablespoon cola

Shake with ice and strain into old-fashioned glass over ice cubes.

PUNCH-À-CRÈME

6 oz white rum
3 oz dark rum
1 egg
6 oz condensed milk
6 oz evaporated milk

Whisk all ingredients together. Serve in short glasses over ice cubes. Serves 6.

RUM & COCONUT WATER

1 oz rum over ice topped with fresh coconut water/milk.

RUM & COKE (Cuba Libre)

1 oz rum over ice topped with Coke in a highball glass or mug.

Add a squeeze of lime or lemon. Garnish with an orange slice.

RUM & GINGER ALE

1 oz rum over ice topped with ginger ale.

RUM & TONIC

1½ oz white rum over ice cubes in a highball glass.

Fill with tonic water and add a squeeze of lime or lemon.

RUM & WATER

1½ oz rum over ice cubes in an old-fashioned glass topped with plain water.

RUM COLLINS

2 oz amber rum
Juice of 1 lime
1 teaspoon powdered sugar

Shake with ice and strain into Collins glass. Add several cubes of ice, fill with soda water and stir. Decorate with a slice of lemon and a cherry. Serve with a straw.

RUM DAISY

1½ oz light rum
¾ oz raspberry syrup
Juice of ½ lemon

Shake and strain into a goblet filled with cracked ice. Add soda and garnish with fruit. Serve with a straw.

RUM DUBONNET

1½ oz light rum
1½ teaspoons Dubonnet
1 teaspoon lemon juice

Shake with ice and strain into a cocktail glass.

RUM FRAPPÉ

Place 1 scoop orange or lemon sherbet in a champagne glass and cover with rum as desired. Stir and serve.

RUM RICKEY

1½ oz light rum
Juice of ½ lime

Pour into a highball glass over ice cubes and fill with carbonated water and ice cubes. Stir and add a wedge of lime.

RUM SCREWDRIVER

1½ oz light rum
3 oz orange juice
Pinch of sugar (optional)

Pour rum over ice cubes in highball glass. Add the orange juice and sugar, if used, and stir lightly. Serve with a slice of orange.

RUM SOUR

2 oz amber rum
Juice of ½ lemon
½ teaspoon powdered sugar

Shake well with ice and strain into a sour glass. Decorate with a half slice of lemon and a cherry.

SANTA CRUZ RUM DAISY

2 oz light rum
Juice of ½ lemon
3 dashes of simple syrup
3 dashes Maraschino or Curaçao

Shake well together and strain into a goblet ⅓ full of shaved ice. Serve decorated with cherries.

SANTIAGO

2 oz amber rum
2 dashes Grenadine
4 dashes lime juice

Stir well with ice and strain into a cocktail glass.

SHARK'S TOOTH

1½ oz light rum
¾ oz 151° proof rum
¾ oz lemon juice
¾ oz lime juice
Dash simple syrup
Dash Grenadine

Pour into a large glass with ice. Top with soda and serve with a straw.

SPANISH TOWN

2 oz amber rum
1 teaspoon Triple Sec

Shake with ice and strain into a cocktail glass. Serve with a grating of nutmeg.

SUFFERING BASTARD

3 oz dark rum
1½ oz light rum
Juice of 1 lime
¾ oz Mai-Tai mix (or make your own – ½ Curaçao, ½ Orgeat)
½ teaspoon powdered sugar

Shake with ice and strain into a large old-fashioned glass about ⅓ full of crushed ice. Garnish with a strip of cucumber rind.

TRINIDAD SWIZZLE

1 oz dark rum
1 oz amber rum
1 oz Grand Marnier
¼ oz lime juice
2 dashes Grenadine syrup
½ oz mango juice
Sugar cane stick
Cherry
Sprig of mint
Slice of orange

Shake liquids with crushed ice, then pour into a tropical glass. Add more crushed ice, and garnish with a slice of orange, the cherry and sugar cane stick.

VIRGIN ISLANDS CREME PUNCH

10 oz white rum
2 bottles beer
6 eggs
2½ tins condensed milk
1½ tins evaporated milk
Juice of 1 lime
3 teaspoons Angostura bitters
½ teaspoon nutmeg
1 teaspoon vanilla

Whip eggs with lime. Add rum, milk and bitters and blend well. Add beer, stir lightly and serve over crushed ice. Garnish with a twist of lime peel or lime slices. Serves 20.

SURPRISED

3 oz amber rum
1½ oz Kummel
1½ oz orange juice
1 dash pimento dram

Shake well with shaved ice and strain into cocktail glasses.

TRINIDAD

2 oz dark Trinidad rum
Juice of ½ lime
3 dashes Angostura bitters
1 teaspoon powdered sugar

Shake well with ice and strain into a cocktail glass.

VIRGIN ISLANDS TWIST

1 oz amber rum
1 oz pineapple juice
¼ teaspoon Grenadine
¼ teaspoon Maraschino

Shake with ice and pour into a cocktail glass.

WELCOME SHADE

2 oz Jamaica rum
2 oz lemon juice
1 teaspoon peppermint
1 teaspoon sugar syrup

Shake vigorously with a lot of ice. Pour into a very tall glass over two or three maraschino cherries. Decorate with mint sprig, slice of orange and slice of lemon, a long spiral of orange peel and a parasol.

WEST INDIAN PUNCH
(For a Crowd)

2 quarts rum
⅕ (25.6 ounces) crème de banane
1 quart pineapple juice
1 quart orange juice
1 quart lemon juice
¾ cup powdered sugar
1 teaspoon grated nutmeg
1 teaspoon cinnamon
½ teaspoon grated cloves
6 oz carbonated water

Dissolve sugar and spices in carbonated water. Pour into large punch-bowl over block of ice and add remaining ingredients. Stir gently and decorate with sliced bananas.

YELLOW BIRD

1½ oz amber rum
¾ oz crème de banane
¼ oz apricot brandy
3 oz pineapple juice
¼ oz orange juice
Dash of Galliano

Shake well with ice and serve in a tall glass.

ZOMBIE

2 oz light rum
1 oz dark rum
½ oz 150° proof Demerara rum
½ oz apricot brandy
½ oz lemon juice
½ teaspoon powdered sugar
1 teaspoon papaya nectar and/or
1 bar spoon pineapple juice and/or
1 bar spoon passion-fruit juice and/or
1 bar spoon plum or apricot juice
Shaved ice and cracked ice

Fill 14 oz zombie glass with shaved ice. Put all ingredients except Demerara rum into a cocktail shaker. Shake well with cracked ice. Pour unstrained into zombie glass. Decorate with sprig of mint or pineapple spear and cherry. Top with Demerara rum, pouring over the back of a bar spoon so that it floats on the surface of the drink. Serve with straws.

BRANDY AND LIQUEUR BASED DRINKS

ANTIGUA STINGER

1½ oz pimento liqueur
1½ oz grapefruit juice
2 oz club soda

Pour pimento liqueur and grapefruit juice into a highball glass with ice. Add club soda and stir lightly.

BAHAMA ROYAL

1 oz coconut rum
1 oz dark rum
2 oz pineapple juice
2 oz orange juice
¼ oz Nassau Royal
2 teaspoons Grenadine

Mix well together and pour into a highball glass with ice. Garnish with a maraschino cherry.

BAHAMAS COW

1½ oz Rumona rum liqueur
2 cups ice-cold milk
1 egg

Whisk the egg into the cold milk until it is thoroughly mixed, then pour the creamy mixture into a tall glass with the Rumona. Stir gently and serve.

BANANA BLISS

1½ oz banana rum
1½ oz brandy

Mix together and serve over ice.

BANANA BOAT

1½ oz banana rum
1 oz sweet sherry
Juice of ½ lime
Ginger ale

Pour ingredients into a highball glass over ice cubes and stir. Fill with ginger ale.

BANANA HOP

2 oz banana rum
6 oz milk
1 egg
1 teaspoon powdered sugar

Shake with ice and strain into a Collins glass. Sprinkle nutmeg on top.

BANANA MAN

1½ oz banana rum
Juice of 1 lime
1 teaspoon powdered sugar
1 tablespoon passion fruit juice

Shake with ice and strain into a cocktail glass.

BANANA SONG

¾ oz banana rum
¾ oz sweet vermouth
4 dashes apricot brandy
2 dashes Grenadine
4 dashes lemon juice

Shake well with ice and strain into a cocktail glass.

BANANA TWIST

1 oz banana rum
1 oz Curaçao
1 oz fresh cream

Shake well with ice and strain into a cocktail glass.

BARBADOS HOP

1 oz brandy
½ oz bourbon
½ oz rum
1 tablespoon powdered sugar
Juice of 1 lemon
Carbonated water

Shake all ingredients except carbonated water with ice. Strain into a Collins glass with ice cubes. Fill with carbonated water and stir.

BARBADOS SOUR

1½ oz cognac
¾ oz pimento liqueur

Shake well with cracked ice and pour into a cocktail glass.

BEACHBANGER

1 oz orange liqueur
1 oz amber rum
½ oz lime juice
Soda or tonic water

Shake orange liqueur, rum and lime juice well with ice cubes and pour into a highball glass. Top with soda water or tonic water. Stir gently and serve.

BERMUDA HIGHBALL

¾ oz brandy
¾ oz dry vermouth
¾ oz dry gin
Ginger ale or carbonated
   water

Pour brandy, vermouth and
gin into a highball glass over
ice cubes. Fill with ginger ale
or carbonated water. Add a
twist of lemon peel, if
desired, and stir.

BETWEEN-THE-SHEETS

¾ oz brandy
¾ oz Cointreau
¾ oz light rum

Shake well with ice and strain
into a cocktail glass.

BLACK PEARL

1 oz Rumona rum liqueur
1 oz cognac
Champagne

Part fill a champagne glass
with cracked ice. Pour in the
Rumona and cognac and top
up to the brim with cham-
pagne. Garnish with a black
cherry.

BLENDERS ROCK

1 oz coconut rum
1 oz 150° rum
1 oz pineapple juice
½ oz lemon juice
½ oz Grenadine
½ oz pineapple rum

Mix well with ice and pour
into cocktail glasses. Garnish
with a slice of pineapple.

BLUE MOON

⅙ amber rum
²⁄₆ Blue Mountain coffee
   liqueur
³⁄₆ milk
Bitters
Ripe banana
1 cup cracked ice

Pour cracked ice into a blender and add the ingredients.
Use one medium-size ripe
banana to each pint of milk.
Blend for two to three
minutes until ingredients are
smooth and foaming then
pour into cocktail glasses.
Add a dash of bitters. Sprinkle
lightly with nutmeg or grated
coconut and serve.

BOSOM CARESSER

1 oz brandy
½ oz Curaçao
Yolk of 1 egg
1 teaspoon Grenadine

Shake well with ice and strain
into a cocktail glass.

BRANDY ALEXANDER

1 oz brandy
1 oz crème de cacao
1 oz fresh cream
Nutmeg

Shake well with ice and strain
into a cocktail glass. Serve
with nutmeg sprinkled on top.

BROWN COW

1 oz Jamaican coffee liqueur
Fresh milk

Pour coffee over ice in a highball glass. Fill with fresh milk
and serve. As a special treat,
add nutmeg.

CARNIVAL

¾ oz brandy
¾ oz apricot brandy
¾ oz Lillet
1 dash Kirsch
1 dash orange juice

Shake with ice and strain into
a cocktail glass.

CAYMAN GIRL

¾ oz Curaçao
¾ oz amber rum
¾ oz fresh cream

Shake well with ice and strain
into a cocktail glass.

CHARLES COCKTAIL

1½ oz sweet vermouth
1½ oz brandy
1 dash bitters

Shake with ice and strain into an old-fashioned glass over ice cubes.

CHERRY BLOSSOM

1½ oz cherry brandy
1 oz brandy
1 dash Curaçao
1 dash Grenadine
1 dash lemon juice

Shake together and serve in a cocktail glass.

CIRRHOSIS-ON-THE-SEA

1½ oz Jamaica coffee liqueur
1½ oz Grand Marnier
1½ oz dark rum
12 oz fresh orange juice
1 dash of lime juice

Mix well together in a jug and serve in tall glasses with plenty of ice.

CITY SLICKER

1½ oz brandy
½ oz Curaçao
1 dash Pernod

Shake well with ice and strain into a cocktail glass.

COFFEE COCONUT

1 oz Jamaican coffee liqueur
2 oz brandy
Nutmeg
1 coconut

Take top off coconut and remove milk/water. Shake half the milk, coffee liqueur and brandy with ice. Strain back into the coconut. Dust with nutmeg and serve with spoon and drinking straws.

COFFEE EGG NOG

2 oz Jamaican coffee liqueur
1 oz brandy
2 oz fresh milk
1 egg (beaten)
1 teaspoon sugar

Blend coffee liqueur, milk and sugar with the beaten egg. Pour over cracked ice and sprinkle with nutmeg. As a nightcap, serve warm. An old-fashioned favourite with a delightful difference.

COFFEE 'N COLA

1½ oz Jamaican coffee liqueur
Cola

Pour the coffee liqueur over
ice in a tall glass. Fill with
cola and serve.

COFFEE-ON-THE-ROCKS

Pour a generous measure of
Jamaican coffee liqueur over
ice. For a little zip, add a
touch of vodka.

COOL MULE

1 oz Jamaican coffee liqueur
1 oz amber rum
1 scoop vanilla ice cream

Blend until smooth and frothy.
Pour into a tall glass and
serve with a cherry.

CUBANA

2 oz brandy
1 oz apricot brandy
1 oz lime juice

Shake well with ice and strain
into a cocktail glass.

DESPERATE VIRGIN

2 oz coconut rum
1 oz 151° rum
2 oz orange juice
1½ oz pineapple or grape-
   fruit juice
½ oz Grenadine

Shake well with ice and strain
into cocktail glasses. Garnish
with lots of cherries.

DOMINICAN FESTIVAL

¾ oz apricot brandy
¾ oz crème de cacao
¾ oz fresh cream
1 teaspoon Grenadine

Shake well with ice and strain
into a large cocktail glass.

DR'S DELIGHT

¾ oz orange liqueur
¾ oz brandy
¾ oz crème de cacao
White of 1 egg

Shake well with ice and strain
into a cocktail glass.

EAST INDIA

1½ oz brandy
½ oz pineapple juice
½ oz Curaçao
1 dash Angostura bitters

Stir well with ice and strain
into a cocktail glass.

FLAMING FLAMINGO

½ oz Grenadine
½ oz green crème de menthe
½ oz Triple sec
½ oz cognac

Pour each ingredient into a
sherry glass in the sequence
given to produce levels of
colour. Set the cognac ablaze
and serve.

FLOATER

1 oz cognac
3 oz mineral water

Pour into a wine glass. The
mineral water will make the
cognac float to the top.

GRASSHOPPER

1 oz green crème de menthe
1 oz white crème de cacao
1 oz fresh cream

Shake well with ice and strain
into a champagne glass.

GRENADIER

2 oz brandy
1 oz Jamaican ginger ale
1 dash Jamaican ginger
1 teaspoon powdered sugar

Stir well with ice and strain
into a highball glass over ice.

GRIM CHASER

½ oz Grand Marnier
½ oz Curaçao
½ oz lemon juice
½ oz Grenadine

Stir well with ice and strain
into a cocktail glass.

HORSE'S NECK

1½ oz brandy
2 dashes Angostura bitters
1 lemon
Dry ginger ale

Peel the skin of the lemon in one piece. Place one end of the peel over the edge of a 10 oz highball glass, giving the effect of a horse's neck. Fill glass with ice cubes. Add brandy and Angostura bitters, top with dry ginger ale. Stir lightly and serve.

JAMAICA COW

1½ oz Rumona rum liqueur
Fresh milk

Pour Rumona into highball glass over ice cubes. Top up with milk, and stir lightly and serve.

JAMAICA HOP

¾ oz Jamaican coffee liqueur
¾ oz white crème de cacao
¾ oz fresh cream

Shake well with ice and strain into a cocktail glass.

LOLLIPOP GIRL

3 oz Cointreau
3 oz Chartreuse
3 oz Kirsch
1 dash Maraschino

Shake well with ice and strain into cocktail glasses. Serve after dinner.

LULLABY BABY

2 oz coconut rum
1 oz Matusalem
2 oz pineapple juice
½ oz lemon juice
½ oz simple syrup

Shake well with ice. Strain over ice in a highball glass and garnish with a slice of orange.

ORANGE BAY

1½ oz orange liqueur
Jamaican dry ginger ale

Pour the orange liqueur over ice in a highball glass. Top up with dry ginger ale. Decorate with an orange slice and serve.

ORANGE BLOSSOM

1½ oz orange liqueur
1 oz vodka
1 oz rum
3 oz orange juice
4 oz pineapple juice

Shake well with crushed ice. Serve over ice in highball glasses.

ORANGEOUTANG

½ oz Wild Orange liqueur
1 oz dry gin
½ oz lemon juice
1 dash bitters

Shake with ice cubes until frost forms. Strain into a tall glass with ice. Garnish with a slice of orange and serve.

PILOT HOUSE HOTEL PIÑA COLADA

1½ oz amber rum
¾ oz coconut rum
3 oz pineapple juice
2 oz evaporated milk
Dash of simple syrup

Shake well and strain into a tall glass with ice.

PIMENTO SOUR

1½ oz pimento liqueur
¾ oz fresh lemon juice
2 oz club soda

Pour over ice in a highball glass. Stir lightly and serve.

RUMONA AND ORANGE

1 oz Rumona
4 oz orange juice

Pour over ice in a highball glass, stir lightly and serve.

RUMONA FRAPPÉ

Pack a cocktail glass with crushed ice and add Rumona rum liqueur.

ST LUCIA JUMP-UP

1½ oz pimento liqueur
1½ oz pineapple juice
2 oz club soda

Pour over ice in a highball glass and serve.

SANGSTER'S DELIGHT

1 oz Blue Mountain coffee liqueur
1 bar spoon simple syrup
1 dash lime juice
1 ripe banana

Blend with crushed ice until smooth. Serve in a brandy snifter with a short straw.

STINGER

1½ oz brandy
1½ oz green crème de menthe

Shake brandy and crème de menthe well with ice. Strain into 3 oz cocktail glass and serve.

TIA ALEXANDRA

¾ oz Jamaican coffee liqueur
¾ oz cognac
¾ oz fresh cream

Shake with cracked ice and strain into a cocktail glass. A remarkably smooth and delicious drink.

T'N'T

1½ oz Tia Maria coffee liqueur
Tonic water

Pour Tia Maria over ice in a tall glass. Top up with tonic. Garnish with lemon slice, if desired.

TROPICAL COFFEE

1 oz Jamaican coffee liqueur
1 oz lime juice
4 oz tonic water

Pour ingredients into a highball glass filled with ice. Garnish with a slice of lime.

WHITE RUM AND SORREL LIQUEUR

To make sorrel, pour boiling water over ½ lb of sorrel flowers from which the petals have been removed. Cool, strain and sweeten to taste. Mix this with one pint white rum and let it steep for a few days. Add Jamaican ginger to taste and drink as an after-dinner liqueur.

WHITE RUSSIAN

¾ oz coffee liqueur
¾ oz vodka
¾ oz fresh milk

Shake well with cracked ice and strain into a cocktail glass.

WHITE SWAN

1½ oz pimento liqueur
3 oz fresh milk

Pour over crushed ice in blender and blend until smooth. Serve in a champagne glass.

GIN, VODKA AND TEQUILA BASED DRINKS

GIN

ALLEN SPECIAL

1½ oz dry gin
½ oz Maraschino
1 dash lemon juice

Stir well with ice and strain
into a cocktail glass.

ATTA BOY

1½ oz dry gin
½ oz dry vermouth
4 dashes Grenadine

Stir well with ice and strain
into a cocktail glass. Serve
with a twist of lemon peel.

BARBADOS APRICOT COCKTAIL

1 oz gin
½ oz apricot brandy
½ teaspoon Grenadine
2 drops bitters
¼ teaspoon lemon juice
Cracked ice

Shake gin, apricot brandy,
Grenadine, bitters and lemon
juice with ice. Strain into a
2½ oz cocktail glass and
serve.

BEER CUP

1½ oz gin
1 bottle Red Stripe beer
Juice of ½ lemon
1 bottle Jamaica ginger beer
Soda water
Slices of cucumber

Mix together beer, gin, ginger beer and lemon juice and
a splash of soda water. Add
ice and stir slightly. Garnish
with a cucumber slice and a
sprig of mint. Serve in 6 oz
glasses. Serves 4.

BERMUDA BOUQUET

1½ oz dry gin
1 oz apricot brandy
1 teaspoon Grenadine
1 teaspoon powdered sugar
½ teaspoon Triple Sec
Juice of ½ lemon
Juice of ¼ orange

Shake with ice and strain into
a highball glass with ice
cubes.

BERMUDA BRONX

3 oz gin
1½ oz dry vermouth
1½ oz sweet vermouth
2 oz orange juice

Shake well with ice and strain
into 2 cocktail glasses.

BERMUDIANA ROSE

¾ oz gin
¾ oz apricot brandy
¾ oz Grenadine
¾ oz lemon juice

Shake well with ice and strain
into a cocktail glass.

BLUE CURAÇAO LADY

¾ oz gin
¾ oz blue Curaçao
¾ oz lemon juice
A dash of egg white

Shake well with ice and strain
into a cocktail glass.

CREOLE LADY

1½ oz dry gin
½ teaspoon Grenadine
1 egg white
1 dash orange bitters

Shake with ice and strain into
a cocktail glass.

BAHAMIAN BULLSHOMARY

2 oz vodka
3 oz consommé
3 oz V8 juice
Lemon and Worcestershire sauce to taste

Pour ingredients into a tall glass half filled with cracked ice. Add a dash of garlic salt. Serve before lunch or the morning after.

BANANA PUNCH

2 oz vodka
1½ teaspoons apricot brandy
Juice of ½ lime

Pour into a Collins glass filled with crushed ice. Add tonic water and top with slices of banana and sprigs of mint.

BARBARA
(Russian Bear)

1 oz vodka
1 oz crème de cacao
1 oz fresh cream

Stir well with ice and strain into a large cocktail glass.

BEER BUSTER

1½ oz 100° proof vodka
Ice cold beer
2 dashes Tabasco sauce

Pour vodka into a highball glass and fill up with beer. Add Tabasco sauce and stir lightly.

BLACK RUSSIAN

1½ oz vodka
¾ oz Jamaican coffee liqueur

Pour over ice cubes in an old-fashioned glass. Stir lightly and serve garnished with an orange slice.

BLENHEIM

1½ oz vodka
¾ oz Jamaican coffee liqueur
¾ oz fresh orange juice

Shake with ice and strain into a large cocktail glass.

BLOODY MARY

2 oz vodka
¼ oz lemon juice
2 drops Tabasco sauce
1 dash Worcestershire sauce
3 cubes ice
Tomato juice
Salt and pepper

In 10 oz glass, put Worcestershire sauce, Tabasco sauce and lemon juice. Add salt and pepper. Mix together then add ice cubes and vodka and top with tomato juice. Serve with a swizzle stick or celery stick.

BULL FROG

1½ oz vodka
4 oz limeade

Pour vodka into a tall glass with ice. Fill with limeade and stir.

BULL SHOT

1 oz vodka
2 oz consommé
Celery salt
2 oz tomato juice
1 dash Worcestershire sauce
1 dash Tabasco sauce

Shake vigorously together. Serve with a sprinkling of black pepper in a 6 oz glass.

EGGHEAD

1½ oz vodka
4 oz orange juice
1 egg

Mix in a blender for one minute at medium speed. Pour into a tall glass with ice and serve.

GODMOTHER

1½ oz vodka
1½ oz Amaretto de Saronno

Stir with cracked ice and strain into a large cocktail glass.

HARVEY WALLBANGER

1½ oz vodka
4½ oz orange juice
¾ oz Galliano

Pour vodka into a tall glass filled with ice cubes. Add orange juice and float Galliano on top.

ICE PICK

1½ oz vodka
Lemon-flavoured iced tea

Pour vodka into a tall glass with ice. Top up with iced tea and stir lightly.

JUNGLE JIM

1 oz vodka
1 oz crème de banane
1 oz fresh milk

Pour into a short glass with ice and stir.

KANGAROO

1½ oz vodka
¾ oz dry vermouth

Shake with cracked ice and strain into a cocktail glass. Serve with a twist of lemon peel.

MOSCOW MULE

2 oz vodka
1 oz lemon juice
Jamaican ginger beer
sprig of mint

Pour vodka and lemon juice over ice cubes in a 10 oz glass. Fill up with ginger beer. Decorate with mint and serve.

PINK CRICKETER

3 oz vodka
2 oz bourbon
1½ oz coconut rum liqueur
½ oz Grenadine
4 oz fresh cream

Shake well with ice and strain into cocktail glasses. Serves 4.

ROAD RUNNER

1 oz vodka
½ oz coconut cream
½ oz Amaretto de Saronno
½ scoop crushed ice

Pour ice into blender, add ingredients and blend for 15 seconds. Rim edge of chilled 4½ oz champagne glass with a slice of orange. Dip rim in sugar and nutmeg mixture. Pour cocktail into prepared glass and top with a dash of nutmeg.

RUSSIAN

1½ oz vodka
1½ oz dry gin
1½ oz crème de cacao

Stir well with ice and strain into cocktail glasses.

SALTY DOG

1½ oz vodka
5 oz grapefruit juice
¼ teaspoon salt

Pour into a highball glass over ice cubes. Stir well and serve.

SCREWDRIVER

1½ oz vodka
Orange juice
Slice of orange
1 maraschino cherry

Pour vodka into a 10 oz high-ball glass containing 3 ice cubes and top up with orange juice. Garnish with the slice of orange and cherry and serve.

SEA URCHIN

1½ oz vodka
Grapefruit juice

Pour vodka over ice in a 10 oz highball glass. Top up with grapefruit juice and serve.

SUN STROKE

1½ oz vodka
3 oz grapefruit juice (unsweetened)
¾ oz Triple Sec or Cointreau

Stir together in a short glass filled with ice and serve.

THE MACHETE

1½ oz vodka
Pineapple juice

Pour vodka over ice in a 10 oz highball glass. Top up with pineapple juice and serve.

VODKA MIST

1½ oz vodka
Twist of lemon

Shake vodka and lemon twist well with ice. Serve unstrained in an old-fashioned glass.

VODKA-ON-THE-ROCKS

Pour 1½ oz vodka over 3 ice-cubes in an old-fashioned glass and serve.

VODKA SOUR

2 oz vodka
Juice of ½ lemon
½ teaspoon powdered sugar

Shake with ice and strain into a sour glass. Garnish with a half-slice of lemon and a cherry.

VODKATINI

1½ oz vodka
¾ oz dry vermouth

Mix together with ice and strain into a cocktail glass. Serve with a twist of lemon peel.

VOLCANO

1 oz vodka
½ oz light rum
1½ oz Southern Comfort

Shake with cracked ice and strain into cocktail glasses.

WHITE ELEPHANT

1 oz vodka
1 oz crème de cacao
1 oz milk

Pour into a short glass with ice and stir.

YELLOW FEVER

1½ oz vodka
4 oz lemonade

Pour vodka over ice in a tall glass. Fill with lemonade and stir. Serve with a straw.

TEQUILA

ACAPULCO

1½ oz tequila
1½ oz amber rum
3 oz pineapple juice
¾ oz grapefruit juice

Shake well with ice cubes and strain into cocktail glasses.

BLOODY BULL

1½ oz tequila
¾ oz lemon juice
1 dash Tabasco sauce
1 dash Worcestershire sauce
Bouillon
Tomato juice

Mix tequila, lemon juice and sauces over ice in 10 oz glass. Fill with bouillon and tomato juice, half and half.

HOT PANTS

1½ oz tequila
2 oz peppermint schnapps
1 teaspoon powdered sugar
1 tablespoon unsweetened grapefruit juice

Shake with ice cubes and strain into an old-fashioned glass rimmed with salt.

MARGARITA

1½ oz tequila
¾ oz lime juice
1 teaspoon Triple Sec

Rub the rim of a cocktail glass with citrus rind then spin it in salt. Shake the tequila, lime juice and Triple Sec with crushed ice. Strain into prepared glass.

PICADOR

1½ oz tequila
¾ oz Jamaican coffee liqueur

Stir with cracked ice and strain into a cocktail glass.

MODERN NO. 2

3 oz Scotch whisky
2 dashes dark rum
1 dash Pernod
2 dashes orange bitters
1 dash lemon juice

Stir well with ice and strain into a large cocktail glass. Serve with a cherry.

MORNING GLORY

1½ oz Scotch whisky
White of 1 egg
1 teaspoon powdered sugar
Soda water

Shake Scotch, egg white and sugar, then strain into a high-ball glass with ice. Top with soda water and serve.

OLD-FASHIONED

Pour into a tumbler 1 or 2 teaspoonsful simple syrup and add 1 to 3 dashes of Angostura bitters. Stir to blend them. Add a little rye or bourbon and stir again. Add 2 large ice cubes and stir again. Fill with more whisky nearly to the top. Stir. Add a zest of lemon. Decorate with a cherry and serve with a spoon to stir further.

ROB ROY

1 oz Scotch whisky
1 oz sweet vermouth
1 dash Angostura bitters
1 maraschino cherry

Stir ingredients with ice and strain into a cocktail glass. Add a cherry and serve.

RUSTY NAIL

Pour 2 parts Scotch whisky and 1 part Drambuie over ice in an old-fashioned glass. Serve with a twist of lemon peel.

VANGUARD

1½ oz Scotch whisky
1 oz medium sherry
½ oz Drambuie
Dash of Angostura

Stir in a cocktail mixer with ice, strain and serve with a maraschino cherry.

WHISKY COCKTAIL

2 oz Scotch whisky
½ oz Curaçao
2 dashes Angostura bitters

Stir well with ice and strain into a cocktail glass. Add a cherry and serve.

WHISKY MILK PUNCH

2 oz Scotch whisky
½ pint milk
1½ teaspoons powdered sugar
Nutmeg

Shake Scotch, milk and sugar with ice and strain into a highball glass. Sprinkle nutmeg on top and serve.

WHISKY-ON-THE-ROCKS

Serve 2 oz Scotch whisky in an old-fashioned glass with ice cubes.

WHIZZ BANG

1½ oz Scotch whisky
¾ oz dry vermouth
2 dashes orange bitters
2 dashes Pastis
2 dashes Grenadine

Stir well with ice and strain into a cocktail glass.

WINE BASED AND NON-ALCOHOLIC DRINKS

AMERICANO

1 oz Campari
1 oz Italian vermouth

Pour over cracked ice in an old-fashioned glass. Stir, add a twist of lemon peel and serve.

BAHAMIAN DELIGHT
(Mike's Favourite)

Mix equal parts of Campari and grapefruit juice. Serve with ice and top off with a cherry.

BAMBOO

1 oz sherry
1 oz sweet vermouth
1 dash Angostura bitters

Stir well with ice and strain into a cocktail glass.

BISHOP'S COOLER

3 oz burgundy
¾ oz dark rum
½ oz orange juice
½ oz lemon juice
1 teaspoon powdered sugar
2 dashes Angostura bitters

Place in a large highball glass and fill with shaved ice. Stir well and serve.

BLACK POWER

2 oz Marsala (dessert wine)
Cola
Slice of lemon

Pour Marsala over ice cubes in an old-fashioned glass. Top up with cola. Add the slice of lemon and serve.

BOO BOO'S SPECIAL

3 oz pineapple juice
3 oz orange juice
Juice of ¼ lemon
1 dash Angostura bitters
1 dash Grenadine
Pineapple wedge or fruit in season.

Shake well with ice and pour into a tall highball glass. Garnish with pineapple or fruit in season.

BRAZIL

1½ oz dry sherry
1½ oz dry vermouth
1 dash Angostura bitters
1 dash Pastis

Stir with ice and serve with a twist of lemon peel.

BUCK'S FIZZ

3 oz orange juice
Champagne

Put cold orange juice into a tall glass. Fill up with chilled champagne.

CAMPARI AND SODA

Pour 2 oz Campari over ice in a tall glass. Fill with soda and stir.

CARIBBEAN BAMBOO

1½ oz dry sherry
¾ oz dry vermouth
1 dash orange bitters

Stir with ice and strain into a cocktail glass. Add a twist of lemon peel and serve.

CARIBBEAN CHAMPAGNE

½ teaspoon amber rum
½ teaspoon crème de banane
Chilled champagne

Pour rum and banana liqueur into a champagne glass. Fill with champagne and stir lightly. Add a slice of banana and serve.

CASSIS FIZZ

1 oz Cassis syrup
Chilled soda water

Pour Cassis syrup into a flute glass and fill up with chilled soda water. Stir lightly and serve.

GREENBRIAR

2 oz dry sherry
1 oz dry vermouth
1 dash of peach bitters

Stir with ice and strain into a large cocktail glass. Decorate with a sprig of mint.

HUMPTY DUMPTY

1½ oz dry vermouth
½ oz Maraschino

Stir well with ice and strain into a cocktail glass.

JUDY'S PUNCH

2 pints lemonade
2 pints soda water
13 oz lemon cordial
8 dashes Angostura bitters
2 oz Grenadine
Fresh fruit salad or 2 tins of fruit salad

Put fresh or tinned fruit salad into punch bowl. Add cracked ice followed by the remaining ingredients. Mix well and serve with fruit from bowl. Serves 20.

CORONATION

1 oz sherry
1 oz dry vermouth
1 dash Maraschino
2 dashes orange bitters

Stir with ice and strain into a cocktail glass.

CUPID

3 oz sherry
1 egg
1 teaspoon powdered sugar
1 pinch Cayenne pepper

Shake well with ice and strain into a large cocktail glass.

KIR

1 oz crème de cassis
Dry champagne

Pour crème de cassis into a wine glass and fill up with chilled champagne. Stir lightly and serve.

67

LEMONADE

Juice of 1 lemon
2 tablespoons powdered sugar
1 slice lemon
Water

Fill a tall glass with cracked ice. Shake lemon juice and sugar and pour unstrained into glass. Top with water. Garnish with lemon slice and serve with straws.

LIMEADE

Juice of 3 limes
3 teaspoons powdered sugar
1 maraschino cherry
water

Fill tall glass with cracked ice. Add lime juice and sugar, top with water and mix thoroughly. Garnish with cherry and serve with straws.

MARIA

2 oz sweet sherry
1 oz dry gin

Stir with ice cubes and strain into cocktail glass. Decorate with a maraschino cherry and serve.

MICKEY MOUSE

Cola
1 scoop vanilla ice cream
Whipped cream

Pour cola into a tall glass with ice. Add ice cream and top with whipped cream. Serve with 2 cherries, drinking straw and spoon.

PANTOMIME

1½ oz dry vermouth
1 egg white
1 dash Grenadine
1 dash Orgeat syrup

Shake well with ice and strain into a cocktail glass.

RAIL SPLITTER

Juice of ½ lemon
1 oz simple syrup
Jamaican ginger beer

Pour lemon juice and syrup into a tall glass with ice. Fill up with ginger beer and stir well.

SHERYL TWIST

1 oz dry sherry
1 oz orange juice
½ oz Scotch whisky
2 dashes Cointreau

Shake with ice and strain into a cocktail glass.

SPRITZER

3 oz Rhine wine
3 oz soda water

Place 1 ice cube in a flute glass. Add Rhine wine and fill up with soda water.

SUMMER FIZZ

12 sprigs mint
1 cup currant jelly
1 cup boiling water
1 cup cold water
3 cups orange juice
½ cup lemon juice
1 bottle ginger ale

Crush mint in a bowl and add boiling water and currant jelly. When jelly is melted, add cold water. Leave to cool. When cold, strain into punch bowl. Add fruit juices and block of ice. Just before serving, pour in ginger ale, stir and decorate with fresh mint. Serves 8.

TEETOTALLERS' PUNCH

26 oz dry ginger ale
26 oz lemonade
13 oz cola
3 oz lemon juice
10 dashes Angostura bitters
Lemon slices

Mix all ingredients with cracked ice in punch bowl. Add lemon slices and serve. Serves 15.

THE FRENCH CONNECTION

3 oz champagne
1½ oz dry gin
Juice of ½ lemon
1 teaspoon powdered sugar

Shake gin, lemon juice and sugar with ice. Strain into 12″ highball glass containing ice. Fill with champagne and serve with a twist of lemon.

HOT DRINKS AND PICK-ME-UPS

BLUE MOUNTAIN PUNCH

3 pints warmed Red Stripe beer
5 oz rum
1 teaspoon powdered Jamaican ginger
3 eggs
2 tablespoons molasses
1 teaspoon grated nutmeg

Blend ginger and nutmeg with 2½ pints beer. Beat eggs with remaining ½ pint beer and the molasses. Mix the two together gradually, beating all the time. Add the rum, beat again and serve. Serves 8.

CAFÉ AU MIKE

1½ oz Jamaican coffee liqueur
¼ oz white crème de menthe
Hot coffee
Whipped cream

Pour the coffee liqueur and crème de menthe into an 8 or 10 oz pedestal mug, fill to within an inch of the rim with a rich full-bodied coffee. Top with whipped cream.

CAFÉ CALYPSO

4 cups freshly percolated coffee
4 oz dark rum
6 oz Rumona rum liqueur
Whipped cream

Blend the Rumona and rum gently with the hot coffee in a heat-proof jug. Serve in large coffee cups, sweetening slightly, if desired. Top with whipped cream.

CARIB-IRISH COFFEE

Black coffee
2 tablespoons Rumona rum liqueur
2 teaspoons castor sugar
Whipped cream

Rinse a large wine glass with warm water, put in sugar and fill glass about ⅔ full with hot, strong, black coffee. Stir. Add Rumona and top with whipped cream.

COFFEE À LA BLUE MOUNTAIN

1 oz brandy
½ oz 151° proof rum
1 oz Jamaican coffee liqueur
½ oz Curaçao
Hot coffee
Whipped cream

Dip the rim of a 14 oz hurricane glass into sugar. Pour in the brandy, rum, coffee liqueur and Curaçao. Fill to within an inch of the top with rich, full-bodied coffee and top with whipped cream.

COFFEE CARIBBEAN

1 oz orange liqueur
1 oz Courvoisier
Hot coffee
Whipped cream

Pour the orange liqueur and Courvoisier into an 8 or 10 oz pedestal mug, fill to within an inch of the rim with a rich, full-bodied coffee. Top with whipped cream.

FESTIVAL PUNCH

1 quart dark rum
1 quart sweet apple cider
2 or 3 sticks cinnamon, broken
2 teaspoons ground pimento (allspice)
1 or 2 tablespoons butter

Heat ingredients in a heavy saucepan until almost boiling. Pour into warm mugs and serve hot. Serves 10.

GLOGG

2 bottles wine (port, sherry,
   claret, burgundy or
   madeira)
1/5 (25.6 oz) brandy
1 lb blanched almonds
1 lb seedless raisins
1 lb lump sugar
2 oz dried orange peel
2 oz cinnamon sticks (broken)
20 cardamom seeds
25 cloves

Tie orange peel, cinnamon
sticks, cardamom seeds and
cloves into a cheese-cloth
bag. Pour the wine into a
heavy saucepan, add spice
bag and boil slowly for 15
minutes, stirring occasionally.
Add the raisins and almonds
and continue to boil for an
additional 15 minutes.
Remove pan from stove and
place wire rack over it. Place
the sugar on the rack and
pour the brandy over it,
making sure to saturate all of
it. Light sugar and let it
flame. After sugar has
melted, cover it with pan lid
to extinguish flame. Stir again
and remove spice bag. Serve
hot in punch cups with a few
almonds and raisins. Serves
12 to 15.

GROG

1½ oz dark rum
1 tablespoon strained lemon
   or lime juice
1 teaspoon simple syrup or
   molasses
Very hot water

Stir rum, lemon or lime juice
and syrup together in an 8 oz
mug. Fill up with very hot
water. Garnish with a twist of
lemon peel and serve.

HOT BARBADOS RUM
EGG NOG

Mix equal measures of rum
and brandy with 1 egg and
1 teaspoonful of sugar in a tall
glass. Fill with hot milk. Stir,
add grated nutmeg and serve.

HOT BUTTERED RUM

3 oz dark rum
1 twist lemon peel
2 sticks cinnamon
1 or 2 cloves
Boiling cider
Butter

Place rum, lemon peel, cloves
and cinnamon in a pewter
tankard or heavy mug. Fill
with boiling cider. Float a pat
of butter on top and stir well
before serving.

HOT BUTTERED RUM
FOR A CROWD

1 lb softened butter
1¼ lb brown sugar
1 cup honey
1 teaspoon grated nutmeg
1 teaspoon ground cinnamon
¼ teaspoon ground cloves
Dark rum
Hot water

Prepare the butter by placing
it in a large bowl with the
sugar, honey, nutmeg, cinnamon, and cloves. Using a
wooden spoon or an electric
mixer, cream these ingredients
until the mixture is completely
blended and fluffy. The butter
will keep refrigerated for
several days. Enough for
about 50 servings. To serve,
pour 1 to 1¼ oz dark rum
into a warmed 8 oz coffee
mug for each serving. Fill
with very hot water and top
with a generous pat of the
spiced butter.

IRISH COFFEE

¾ oz Irish whisky
2 cubes sugar
Hot coffee
Heavy cream whipped with
    sugar to taste

Pour the whisky into a 6 oz pedestal glass over 2 cubes of sugar. Pour the hot coffee down the back of a metal spoon set into the glass to prevent cracking. Remove spoon, top with whipped cream and serve.

JAMAICAN COFFEE

1 oz Jamaican coffee liqueur
¾ oz dark rum
Hot coffee
Grated nutmeg

Pour coffee liqueur and rum into a coffee mug. Add hot coffee and sprinkle with nutmeg.

MADGE

1 oz brandy
1 oz Jamaican coffee liqueur
1 oz crème de cacao
Hot coffee
Whipped cream

Pour the brandy, coffee liqueur and crème de cacao into an 8 or 10 oz pedestal mug, fill to within an inch of the rim with a rich, full-bodied

coffee. Top with whipped cream.

MEXICAN COFFEE

1 oz tequila
1 oz Jamaican coffee liqueur
Hot coffee
Whipped cream
Powdered cinnamon

Pour the tequila and coffee liqueur into an 8 or 10 oz pedestal mug, fill to within an inch of the rim with a rich, full-bodied coffee. Top with whipped cream and sprinkle with cinnamon.

SONS OF NEGUS

Heat 1 bottle of sherry or port and place in a pitcher. Rub a little lemon rind on 6 cubes of sugar and add to heated wine. Add 2 to 3 large twists of lemon rind and the juice of 1 lemon, 10 drops of vanilla and 2 cups of boiling water. Sweeten to taste, if necessary, and strain into glasses. Add a grating of nutmeg and serve. Serves 8.

SPECIAL JAMAICAN RUM PUNCH

1 bottle dark rum
1 bottle brandy
½ bottle sherry
2 lemons
4 oz sugar
1 teaspoonful ginger
Up to 3½ pints boiling water
Grated nutmeg

Grate the rind of the lemons into a small earthenware bowl and add sugar. Macerate sugar and lemon gratings with the juice of the lemons and the ginger. Mix well and place in another large earthenware bowl, previously heated. Add, in the following order, rum, brandy, sherry and boiling water. Stir well, sweeten further if desired, and stand near heat for 20 minutes. Serve in glasses or mugs, with a grating of nutmeg on top. Serves 20.

TODDY

1½ oz brandy, rum or whisky
1 teaspoon simple syrup
1 cinnamon stick
Very hot water

In an 8 oz cup place syrup, brandy, rum or whisky. Fill up with very hot water and serve with a cinnamon stick.

PICK-ME-UPS
For the morning after

CORPSE REVIVER

Shake with ice 1 part brandy, 1 part Fernet Branca and 1 part white crème de menthe. Strain into a glass and serve.

PICK-ME-UP LICK-ME-DOWN COCKTAIL

Shake with ice 1 part cognac, 1 part dry vermouth and 1 part pastis. Strain into a glass and serve.

PRAIRIE OYSTER NO. 1

1½ oz brandy
1 dash Worcestershire sauce
1 egg
Salt, if desired

Carefully break egg into 6 oz glass. Add Worcestershire sauce and brandy. Stir lightly, keeping yolk intact since it has to be swallowed whole.

PRAIRIE OYSTER NO. 2

1 teaspoon Worcestershire sauce
1 teaspoon tomato ketchup
2 dashes lemon juice
2 dashes olive oil
1 egg yolk
Salt and black pepper

Put Worcestershire sauce and ketchup into 4 oz glass. Add egg yolk carefully, keeping it intact, then lemon juice, olive oil and salt and pepper. To be drunk off in one gulp.

SHISKA BOUSKA

1 oz Metaxa
1 lemon slice

Pour the metaxa into a pony glass. Brush the lemon slice with instant coffee and place on top of the glass.

TERMINOLOGY

Blazers Drinks that are set alight. For a brandy blazer, put a lump of sugar, a twist of lemon peel, a twist of orange peel and a lot of brandy into a flame-proof mug or tankard. Light the mixture, stir and strain.

Cobblers Iced and sweetened long drinks with a spirit or wine base. Finely crushed ice goes into the tumbler first, followed by the ingredients with the base liquor going in last.

Collins A refreshing long drink made with Dutch gin is called a John Collins. With Old Tom, it is called a Tom Collins.

Cordials These are sweetened, aromatised spirits and are regarded as heart stimulants.

Fizzes Spirit based long drinks with a form of sweetener. In short, a sour made to fizz with soda water or other aerated waters or sparkling wine.

Frappés Drinks served with broken or crushed ice, as opposed to 'on the rocks'. The ice goes first into a long or medium glass followed by a liqueur and two straws. Crème de menthe frappé complements your supper on a hot summer night.

Highballs Long iced drinks consisting of a base liquid combined with carbonated beverages, but without citrus juices.

Rickeys Spirit based drinks with fresh limes or other fruit if limes are unavailable. Gin, sloe gin and rum make the best rickeys.

Smashes Mixed iced drinks flavoured with mint.

Sours Spirit based drinks with citrus fruit juice and usually a sweetener. Also called daisies, crustas and fixes. Crustas are served cold, the ice remaining in the shaker, while daisies are served 'on the rocks' usually with raspberry syrup for the sweetener. Fruit is added.

Toddies Hot drinks, usually sweetened.

YOUR LIQUOR REFERENCE

Amaretto Italy's delicious almond-flavoured liqueur.

Anisette 44° Sweetened version of Anis. Makes a long drink with bitter lemon, ice and a little lime juice.

Aperitif A drink taken to stimulate one's appetite, usually a wine based cocktail.

Apricot Brandy 42° A highly flavoured liqueur made from apricots.

Benedictine 73° A sweet, herb-flavoured brandy based liqueur. One of the oldest liqueurs in the world and originally made by the Benedictine monks. Can be mixed with equal parts of brandy and is sometimes referred to as D.O.M.

Bitters A blend of roots and herbs used for flavouring. The best known brands are Angostura, Fernet Branca and Peychaud.

Brandy	Distilled from fermented juice of ripe grapes or other fruits. The best of the brandies is cognac.
Calvados	A French apple brandy.
Cherry Brandy 42°	A brandy based on the juice of ripe cherries.
Coconut Cream	Made from freshly grated coconut. It is placed in a cloth in a seive and a cup of hot water for each cup of grated coconut is poured over it. The cloth is wrung out and the liquid left to stand. When it is cool, the cream will rise to the surface and can be skimmed off.
Cointreau 70°	A sweet, colourless liqueur with orange flavour.
Coconut rum	Based on the juice of the coconut and fine rum.
Coconut liqueur	A delightful liqueur made from the juice of the coconut blended with spirits.
Crème de banane	A yellow brandy based liqueur flavoured with bananas.
Crème de cacao	A very sweet dark liqueur made from cocoa beans, vanilla and spices.
Crème de cassis	A liqueur with blackcurrant flavour.
Crème de menthe	A peppermint-flavoured liqueur in green, white or red.
Dubonnet	A dark red French aperitif with a red wine base and a slight quinine taste.
Galliano 70°	A gold-flecked liqueur with liquorice and anisette flavour.
Gin	Alcohol made from any source of sugar. Tasteless until re-distilled with juniper berries, coriander seeds, angelica root, calemus, cardamom seeds and orris powder, the principal flavouring ingredients.
Grand Marnier	French brandy liqueur with orange flavour; brown in colour.
Grenadine	Red promegrante flavouring used as a sweetener.
Green Ginger Wine	Wine made from fruit and Jamaican ginger.
Lillet	A French aperitif with a white wine base.
Mango Juice	Juice made from the mango fruit.
Maraschino 45°	A colourless, cherry-flavoured liqueur from Italy and Yugoslavia.
Orange Bitters 70°	Made from the peel of bitter Seville oranges. Much used in flavourings.
Papaya Juice/ Syrup	Made from the juice of the papaya fruit.
Peach Brandy	A brandy-coloured liqueur with peach flavour.
Pimento Liqueur	A liqueur made from the berries of the pimento tree which is to be found only in Jamaica. A sharp, biting, spicy taste.
Rumona	A liqueur with Jamaican rum base.
Schnapps 66.5°	Scandinavian liqueur made from potatoes and flavoured with caraway seeds.
Triple Sec	White Curaçao. A colourless liqueur with a sweet orange flavour.
Tequila 66.5°	A Mexican drink made from pulque, a fermented drink produced from the sap of the cactus plant, also called century plant, agave, mescal. The Mexican way to drink it is 'a lick of salt from the back of the hand and a sip of the tequila'.
Vodka	An alcoholic distillate from a fermented mash of grain. It is colourless.
Whisky	A spirit obtained from the distillation of a fermented mash of grain i.e. barley, maize or rice, mainly, and aged in wood.

INDEX